NIGHTHAWKS AND IRISES

NIGHTHAWKS AND IRISES

Poems About Paintings

Robert Kirschten

Mellen Poetry Press
Lewiston•Queenston•Lampeter

Library of Congress Cataloging-in-Publication Data

Kirschten, Robert, 1947-
    Nighthawks and irises : poems about paintings / Robert Kirschten.
        p. cm.
    ISBN 0-7734-3418-6 (pbk.)
    1. Painting--Poetry. I. Title

PS3561.I773 N5   2000
811'.54--dc21

00-057871

The Edwin Mellen Press   The Edwin Mellen Press
Box 450   Box 67
Lewiston, New York   Queenston, Ontario
USA 14092-0450   CANADA L0S 1L0

The Edwin Mellen Press, Ltd.
Lampeter, Ceredigion, Wales
UNITED KINGDOM SA48 8LT

Printed in the United States of America

CONTENTS

EDWARD HOPPER'S PAINTING "NIGHTHAWKS, " 1942
Art Institute, Chicago

You find no filament
illuminating this 1940's all-night cafe
with its incandescent ceiling
blazing
in a scalene horizontal
of pale yellow.
Instead of electric globes,
your eye encounters spectral glare
flung outward in wedges
as if beaming from
above three lone patrons:
one back-turned faceless fedora
at the counter
and a couple with fixed gaze
of aluminum coffee urns.
For Hopper's light radiates coldly
from within forms,
not from the unseen street lamp
or fluorescent tubes,
but within these blue-streaking shadows
pointing inside
from the pavement
like a string of fallen pennants.
Even as the starched late-shift attendant
bends toward empty stools, his uniform reflects
only the artist's austere harmony
of faded whites with
the hour's dazzling numbness.
If you peer closer,
what you thought a plate glass window,
like familiar laws of light,
vanishes
into Hopper's framing
of that neon corner grill you pass,
not noticing
these same glazed stares,
perched nightly
in vitreous isolation.

EDWARD HOPPER'S PAINTING "GAS," 1940

I.

This is the question I told you not to ask:
whether or not the station attendant in vest and tie at the rack
of oil cans hears you is incidental;

he will not respond.

He will not turn to face you even if you ask him to avert your gaze
from the bleak road of inquiry behind his back.

You cannot stop here for gas.

The horizontal thrusts of gray highway, green forest, blue sky,
and burnt firegrass drive your eye right
past
the carved pumpkin face of the ghostly gas station
and its sheet-white skin of wooden slats,
with the unseen candle, inside, burning flashlight-yellow
to set the stage for

the skeletal fingers of bone-bright light, outside, that cannot
reach quite far
enough
to the road to clutch you for asking.

II.

Try and rephrase the question. That will not work either, as you
begin to feel more vacant than before.

The firegrass that flames under the feet of the forest fuels
the burning route yet will not
consume it.

Even if you don't believe that the triangle of gas pumps is three-
headed Cerebus, guard dog to Hades at a gas station,
these three globe-eyes--crowning the pump tops with magnifying
circles,

their logos white-washed off with light,
each with a red-winged Pegasus for horse-power
ascending to the sky--
accelerate
the slant downward down the road into the vaginal dark,
toward the unliteral word
that continues to drive you, with or
without
the question.

III.

Go ahead, and laugh.   Laugh all you want, while you're running on
empty,
running
toward a myth you can't foresee as myth, the only kind
you can believe--and live.

Part of the answer is that the red-stockinged, one-legged sign
is a gate, that the attendant is the gatekeeper, that the gate
is raised,
that the road is clear,
that the hoze-arms on the pumps are locked in upright position,
unavailable
to flag down any car racing alone,
just as the blank semaphore on the roofless outhouse
is irrelevant to gender.

You are not completely lost.

What is available is Hopper's only word
about the magical momentum between energy and enervation.
Below a fourth winged horse of fire engine red,
brightly-lit upon
the portal
high above his entrance into eternal night,

Hopper's clear, blue-lettered emblem for all your travels:

Mobilgas.

3

EDWARD HOPPER'S PAINTING
"LIGHTHOUSE AT TWO LIGHTS," 1929

I. At First Light

This vanilla-white lighthouse tower looks, at first,
in Hopper's bright sun,
like a weathered, New England ice cream cone, upside down,
with two scoops,
one for each catwalk, under
the top-coating of the cupola itself with bulb.
Ascending from seven triangle-trapezoid roofs, flat black,
staggered up the hill like stairs,
left toward the sky-blue
cipher of blue
sky,

this frosting-white barberpole of a snowman
(on top of its wedding-cake white box
pedestal)

is a three-eyed sentinel (with buttons) on the shade side
of the tower,
under the snowman's scarf, the lower catwalk.

Such winter dressing in summer is, surely, Hopper's sly wash
on how to keep a look out
for the whiteness of whiteness, that stark
metaphysical fear
about the surfaces and depths of divinity,
overlaying the structural center-shaft
of so lucid a comic portrait

about a beacon for ships
at sea

that will always guide us home.

II. At Second Light

No mechanical light, a greater wind of clarity blows from
the right side,
up, far beyond the frame, and all eyes begin to see

what no lost ship will ever seek:

not nature's sun, but light
so bright the lighthouse buildings droop their heavy-lidded shades
half-way in stunned, sleepy squints.

This blinding, binding light, in air too fresh to breathe, slants
slowly into sight against
the walls of buildings, bleached white by Hopper's serene storm
of stasis,

resounding non-motion, radiant with hushed impact of volumes,
chiselled in paint heavy as stone;

grows brighter and brighter and brighter until all stands still,
then slowly, even more slowly, the ground
begins to move,
one barnacle-bush at a time then the entire bottom base
of the composition,

and you begin to understand
that the lighthouse houses are houses of light

--built from the sensations of sun, from the appearance
of appearances, from the divine absence of celestial satisfaction--

that the walls are sails, driving the mast of light that is the tower
before the wake of a silent sea,

that the hill under the house is a hull, and that the earth is moving
the sun past two clouds
like empty ghosts in Halloween sheets
blowing

past the life you forgot to lead, and remember not to celebrate.

This is the white divinity you have always feared, the comic mask you never can remove.

This is the question you were afraid to ask.

EDWARD HOPPER'S WATERCOLOR
"METHODIST CHURCH, PROVINCETOWN," 1930

"The beginning and the end of all literary activity is
the reproduction of the world that surrounds me by means
of the world that is in me."
--Goethe

This quote you carried in your wallet "applies" also
"to painting from memory," you said.

Even though my own far-sighted view of Provincetown
is now the brackish shoal long ago
of all salt water,
my poem about your watercolor flows fresh
from memory in colors,

not from a church
far distant on Cape Cod, but the church you remembered
to paint
from the memory your gaze was radiant
to remember.

If the waters of color rise and swell before me,
the picture of Provincetown
that was in you will--with hope--surround the world
of words surrounding me,

so I write
with hope, and wonder
how you remembered to paint both worlds
from recollection:

white:

I wonder how you remembered to see so many pairs
of eyes in so many square-framed
window frames:

window-eyes, half their shades half-drawn in shade,
the other half, half-alert to the bleach-white
splash of sun all over
their fence-white faces, as though they could not
look beyond your joke
that their sleepy ocean spray of a town
has been white-washed awake
by a clean bright
brush
with your light;

brown, black, and beige:

I wonder how you remembered that these smokeless stacks
sprouted like snorkels out of a shipwreck
of brown,
black, and beige shingles,
each roof-top presuming the submerged mass
of a house's hulking hull, each chimney
hulking its head higher
and higher
to get a better view
of the angled tide of currents, swirling like a school
of brown, black, and beige
sharks
throughout your composition;

violet:

I wonder how you remembered to stack wedge
upon wedge upon triangle up against each other,
triangle after wedge upon
church tower,
until space is flatted into a facade of sharp faces,
until each building aspires to be part
of the body of the church,
aspiring spires,
pushing buttress-like up toward the bifocaled belfry,
while a violent

                    violet horizontal drives the final
                              ascent to

                         water-color cloud:

a fleece flowing full of angels' wings: sky-blue and white again,
         flowing through sky the color of hope flown high
                    through water and color:
     beyond a slow shoal of white, brown, black, beige, and violet:

        in a wash of the ominous and the earth-bound, beyond
                God's serene, azure absence, flowing:
          awash with words and worlds and wonder surrounding me:

        as I remember to paint my memory of Edward Hopper
                          remembering.

VINCENT van GOGH'S "IRISES," 1890

You must guard the water and fire dwelling in the arcane substance
and contain those waters with the <u>aqua permanens</u>, even though
this be no water, but the fiery form of the true water.

--<u>Rose Garden of the Philosophers</u>
(16th Century alchemical text)

You brush each flower into flame.

All across the twisting arc of your bouquet, ice petals of watery
fire
crown the curve
of cobalt-cool, liquid-flowing forms,
swirl-bursting
vastly beyond their fiery sticks of sparklers
into serpent-tongues that burn
to speak
in sapphire tones of the arcane substance of dragon-stone.

Frozen jade stiletto-stalks shoot upward from the pitcher's
pale mouth
of lime-on-white, spitting out
their graceful madness, ready any time, to blossom blades
into the bullet
you fired through your heart or your comic attempt
to kill Gauguin.

God is in the violence.
God is your faith in frenzy you picture-paint over nature's
painted face.

This is no sweet still life. It is rain-water, mercury, salt,
sulphur, consecrated wine--
clouding, combining, becoming, transmuting chaos
into
all that shines.

This is your sublime retort to instability.   This is the suicide's
self-singing song
to his own skulking source of sly serenity.

Deep inside each iris, each vessel, the magic waters boil, bubble,
cross,   curl, and cry out
to the dark womb of their own divinity,
beautiful and lethal,

celebrating each bright secret you guard in water and fire,
even though this be no water.

Each ferments and putrefies
in blue.

Each condenses its miracle of sudden, sullen joy around and around
your dance
of scorching cold
in rings
of jubilant jewels: the alchemist's true, permanent iris:
no fool's gold, but amethyst.

JONATHAN GREEN'S PAINTING "WHITE BREEZE," 1995

O South Carolina island woman,
carry us upward
on your white gown, gulf-streaming across your broad black
shoulders,
like a cape of clouds
white as these wind-brisk curtains billowing free,
blowing
white toward heaven.

As you lift your head, gaze skyward beyond your tilted-up,
brimming laugh
of a discus-platter straw hat,
show us how
its spiralling height and that of these two blue-white eagles
soaring
match your own.

Let your ebony arms muscle-ripple the arcing flight
of black sea birds
up, up and higher in a puff rush
of
cloud-sailing,
black and white, white and black

on Jonathan Green's green ocean white breeze,
where all colors
ascend.

MARY CASSATT'S PAINTING "THE LETTER," 1891

So simple a gesture of suspense:
she moistens the envelope while the message lies folded
on her writing desk.

This elegant woman has no ring on her fingers and few touches
of gray in her hair.
Her expression is opaque yet thoughtful.
Is this the end of a romance
or merely a thank you note for some cautious courtesy?

Has she forgiven a past wrong? Does she write to beg forgiveness?
Might her heart beat in every word?

The design on her dress seems a patterned extension of the flowery
wall paper.
Cassatt has flattened all surfaces.

The letter waits.

WILLIAM MERRITT CHASE'S PAINTING
"AT the SEASIDE," ca. 1892

If this parasol of white satin spins any slower to shake the sun
from this four-cornered, red-tasselled,
orange Victorian sofa-pillow for sitting on sand,
the clouds would
almost
stop strolling through the sky.

Right here.

William Chase dabs them in in dappled-in dreamy dabs
of cool coconut-pudding-pie white
paint
--like cotton-candy, like powder-puffs, like sugar-cubes,
like egg-whites, like cotton-balls--
drifting slowly, slowly drifting in spurts and splashes
on sea breezes
that are really schemes of invisible slices
of 19th Century American
seaside shapes:

triangles twisting slowy like silent wind chimes,
using each angle and aspect of beach umbrellas, bathing dresses,
skiffs, sails, and sun bonnets
to balance the cadence of composition
against
a trio of stacked, horizon-wide wedges,
basking in the quiet calm of three breathlessly unexcited shades
of sky-blue, ocean-blue, and shore-beige gray.

The parasol points Chase's unspinning pinwheel of winds
to a pin cushion-cloud,
an axis, focal point, center-button, a middle for the slip-cover
momentum
below
surf and surfaces,.

which casually mix and mingle, blow and blend,
lively as tea leaves
on this gull-sunny day at the beach, floating
above the first porcelain cup
of conversation.

Right there.

No sea breeze soughs softer, flows smoother, slows sweeter than
the lazy pace
of this impressionist's impressions
--right here, right there--
sailing through the slant spray of sleight brush strokes
all the way across the bay
and back.
Two cartwheel-umbrellas, yellow and orange, finally anchor
this cloudy confection
to its ditty of open salt air, a visual tune, something
Chase shows us
to sing
by the seaside by the beautiful sea.

PAUL CEZANNE'S "STILL LIFE with APPLES," 1895-1900

I have seen the apples there that toss you secrets,--
Beloved apples of seasonable madness
That feed your inquiries with aerial wine.
                              --Hart Crane

Once you stilled a human model, sitting not still enough,
"Does an apple move?"
These do:
These models of apples blossom forth from your table-terrain
of still-spinning spheres,
each on
its axis-stem, turning color almost turning
yellow ochre around red-sienna around madder-red around
burnt orange:
slow-bowling rolling balls
beneath
a blue-white bowl of Veronese green
green apples.

They are stacked, juggled flat, against two table cloths of more
blue-white
pushing up front
the foreground into two-flat dimensions,
where nature's depth is brushed outside your lush world's
opulent orchard,
where some day soon the Cubists
will take their next century's holiday from impressions
from
your fresh-cut fruit.

Higher and slower, slower and stiller, the great stone wheel
of the gathered curtain,
upper left,
grinds to your halt
in mid-air above the glass goblet,
tilted by purple,
that momentarily postpones the crushing confrontation

between
arabesques and apple sauce.

Because you peeled geometry to its core, this angled world
of volumes is designed
by
the argument from design:

you build and balance by sphere, cylinder, cone, plane,
all
the paraphernalia
God uses against gravity
to bring the background closer enough
to keep the apples from falling off the table
into the shapeless banality
of our fruitless lives.

Oh, toss us still your beloved apples, your seasonable secrets,
your full flush fare
of reds and yellows, stiller, still,
still
rich with aerial wine.

CLAUDE MONET'S "LANDSCAPE near ZAANDAM," 1872

This is serenity.

That white canvas sail drifting toward you on the pale river
will never arrive too late
for
you to miss
this slow boat to Zaandam, slide-gliding downsteam
into its own still reflection.

It is always on time.

Don't hurry. Don't rush. This is not tardy sentimentality
to skim the casual clouds
above Monet's watery stream of objects
at your own pace,
as long as you slow-float safely down again
below
the horizon line
of romantic realism.

When these trees of branch-fleeces and wooly leaves bend
their necks for a drink,
the shore houses melt into an orange-lime frappé
of cream-colored ripples,
never
too French to quench
your thirst for thaw from Monet's earlier summer ices
of sharply focused reds and sporty
yellows.

If you see yourself adrift, your color-blind eyes of polished,
lens-angled insight are
in the right place
to drip and dribble reason's wiles away,
away from glum self-steerage,
down this lazy, hazy river, trickling from the tangible
to tangerine.

You could catch the next boat--for destination.
You could pirate the dinghy on the left bank--for direction.
These are far too reliable for rewarding
repose.

Instead, row well below the undertow of Monet's over-flow, quiet
combination
of color and current; go
barge-slow   barnacle-slow   seaweed-slow   clam shell-slow
until
the painter pulls you on board the drift of his dream
to
no-motion slow.

Now you can coast constantly and confidently all along the stopped
serene sheen of sensation.

CLAUDE MONET'S "MORNING on the SEINE near GIVERNY," 1897

"Monet is only an eye, but what an eye!"
                                    --Paul Cezanne

Turn the morning river around upside down; only the painter's
                    eye dissolves
        these waters into the same supple stream of sky,
            where reflection constantly turns,
                    turns the same
                        scene
                    over and over
    before the mind's course sweeps its own swirling currents
                    downstream
            back and forth between the line-straight
                shores of hind-sight.

Monet's mirror-brush wakens morning-freshness to the mystery
                    of mist
                and sensation
            back across the same
        cloud-cluster that ripples between two breadths
            of trees, drifting from bank to bank,
            from shallow to shadow, all along
                    this river
                of shimmering light

                    until
            both halves of nature's sketch
                are wholly half
        water and half the horizon of heaven, the angels' airy
                zone of appearance
    and disappearance, where objects are dream-shaded
                into atmosphere and space
                    into silence.

            Turn the picture. Turn it again.
            What does Monet's eye show you to see?

--mushrooming puffs of green-blue smoke-smog: onion-dome
                                        turrets

20

of violet-yellow tree tops: overhanging crowns of beige-gold
boughs:
the imagination's
contours haunted by the clarifying clash of complementary colors,
giving depth to a Seine of surfaces only
now
you can see
only with your eye, but what an eye!

CLAUDE MONET'S "LA PIE (The Magpie)," 1869

One must have a mind of winter
To regard the frost and the boughs
Of the pine-trees crusted with snow . . .
                    --Wallace Stevens

Magpie, perched alone
along the top wooden rail of this rickety country gate,
is your mind
of winter
black enough against the white snow and the lily pond-purple
                                                shadow
of the woven fence,
reflecting the ice-blue snow-roof of the cottage,
to regard
stark contrasts between colorless colors as the placid frost
from Monet's cool contradictions?

Do you view the forest's black branches as dancing claws
grasping for snow-tufted crowns
of opposites?

Do you remark the foreground path of mottled-dirty specks as
it dazzles
up into a pure cold cream sky,
rushing
toward the hidden sun
after passing
through the entrance gate you guard?

No matter.
This painting is not about you.

GEORGES de La TOUR'S PAINTING
"CHRIST in the CARPENTER'S SHOP," c. 1640

It is almost all dark,
all around the father and son as Joseph bends down building,
perhaps, a chair. He could be bowing, for God is a child
lower than Joseph
but with
the glow of divinity from
a single source
that illumines even the dirt under the child's fingernails
in this benighted carpenter's shop,
where
Christ holds his candle like a tool.

SEBASTIEN STOSKOPFF'S "STILL LIFE of GLASSES in a BASKET,"
1644

It might have been some monarch's knocked-around party crown,
this golden, woven basket,
brim-high,
full
of clattering glass goblets that appear ready to shatter
at any second,
yet make no ringing sound as subtle as
your
not swallowing
the two cracked fragments
in front
of this radiant, sun-king shimmering spectacle
of stillness
from
Sebastien Stoskopff.

PIERRE DUPUYS' PAINTING "BASKET of GRAPES," c. 1650

25

You would love to pluck each and every one off each and every stem
and never find a sour grape
in this small plush structure of pale green leaves,
with purple-black and lime-light pearls
strung
in lush bunches

so somberly fresh that
each grape glistens with its own sweet sweating diamond-dab
of light.

Yet there is this one moment of muted mutability in front
on the cracked terra cotta table:
a single small shape
drying
almost to a raisin
--balanced, life-like, by a ripe-round red apple--
here
where sumptuous humility grows
on a vine.

PIERRE PATEL (the ELDER): "LANDSCAPE with RUINS," c. 1763

I

O incandescent sun of the sublime,
yolk-bursting between two distant madonna-blue mountain peaks,
fire up this entire lacquered earth, even the pastoral
shepherd with his sweet flock,
crossing down across
the arch of brick bridge toward washer women
who wring the stream out
from their egg white sheets far below
regal shards.

Let your decorous explosion tarry long enough before breakfast,
to gild
God's gold-smoldering apocalypse as it readies to dry
terribly more
than the laundry on the line.

II

O you three wrath-riddled Corinthian columns,
let noiseless tumult loom
high above
your straight-up ruined temple-thrust as you prepare to attack
God's bright booming light
head-on.

Stand erect long enough to ignite your bountiful fury
to make hell make love
come alive!

FRANCOIS DAUBIGNY'S "THE BARGES," 1865

Daubigny's barren barge-masts are two fishing poles
with red flags,
trolling the river-sky of clouds
for floating forms
that will not fracture nature's favored fragments
away from
its hourly shifts of light.

Or are these masts slender spindles for the center of his
countryside's
florid wheel
of some lush, blue-green French cheese,
cut
into sketch-like slices
of pasture, shore, water, hulls and banks of brackish branches,
by a starving artist struggling
for structure?

Exactly both.

This is Daubigny's postcard-perfect picture
of a picnic lunch site
for out-doors objects wandering their way above the river
of this painter's tonal impressions:

a visual vacation adrift on a cheese wheel of wedges:
--summer camp and crackers
for the eye--
a postcard mailed home, recording the real in real impressions
revolving
around five flat decks and two straight lines:

all barge-sailing slowly
up
up
fishing for sky.

GEORGIA O'KEEFE'S PAINTING
"MUSIC--PINK and BLUE, II," 1919

Why
does so volatile a flow of obviously feminine forms
make me, a man,
feel, at first, too remote to write with much inwardness
about so melodious a woman's
terrain?

Unlike the sandpaper skin of my own rasping landscape,
everything here streams like silk
scarves
in and around and through
a light airy vapor of sister shapes:
mountains are breasts and lips and labial caves,
surging
like large layered petals of light or parachute-buds
that open up and down into
clouds
of pink and blue and lavender and lime.

O'Keefe makes me veer closer.

A single umbilical swings the rainbow-womb of nature's pulsing
hot air balloon
--one blue-cool oval blasts up the burner of O'Keefe's organic
aether--
so high in her sky
of archetypes that even
I am
swirling and swelling and spinning inward
to see how she gives visual birth to the festive bodies
that give life's music
to us all.

The grass needs cutting.

Wild bouquets of ocher-orange sprays spout-sprout out
almost any direction up
from Manet's lush-fresh rush
of grounds.

No clarifying sky is in view. Jungle darkness lurks slightly
like dank weeds
in shadowy backgrounds
below the horizon of yellow-green tree leaves,
dappled-
dabbling above a bleached stone wall
all along the top frame
of the garden.

Nothing is neat

except the trellis: a lattice-cell of squares to keep your wild eye
inside nature's ardent cage
--together with the wall, it's an ancient aquaduct
with three main arches,
filtering the artist's spatial stream
of fragmented stalks
through left through center through right.

A patch of blanched-white path slowly washes over the park-
green
seat of the park bench
as one porous object picnics around about
another.

Things begin to brighten.

The path's wide thrust of egg-shell sun-white radiates
toward an inviting center

of circles hidden behind the foliage
of its glowing circumference.

A glass decanter on a cafe table
waits there for some glad hand to pour its own
translucent light.

The empty bench is pruned and poised to seat any vacant visitor
looking forward to flower in this garden-harvest
of growth

where
expectation blossoms like a rose.

Now should you enter Eden.

JEAN BAPTISTE-CAMILLE COROT'S "LA DAME en BLEU," 1874

My God, this is drudgery, standing still as a statue. I am the dame
in blue, turning blue, blue with boredom in this courtesan's pose.

If I hold my delicate hand up under my elegant chin much longer,
my right arm, bare and already

half-an-hour asleep with cold, becomes an ice-blue pin cushion
for a porcupine.

Did the artist say the color of my opera gown is cobalt blue,
midnight blue, Prussian blue, or indigo?

I don't care. My fingers are turning bluer than all his tubes
of paint.

How my back aches, but the painter's stare keeps my spine, arcing
straight as the flight of a blue arrow.

I want to go home, uncork the wine, and make love to my boyfriend
Pierre, but I am frozen here, frozen forever in blue.

The great Corot slowly wipes his brush with that smelly rag
in turpentine that oozes

through his dark, stuffy studio and crawls into my every pore.
He tells me

my upper arm is fleshy-fat. "Then paint it thin--and blue!"
I cry back into a face I feel but cannot turn to see.

His scorching eyes --are they blue? I do not want to know--
criss-cross up, down, over, around

the pale skin of my shoulder. Those eyes are not hot hands.
They are fire-cool fingers, folding

and unfolding each pleat in my dress and tensing each muscle
in my neck.

50 years older than I, Grand Pa Pa with those young man's eyes.
My bodice says my body will never bore him.

Even Pierre does not look at me this way.

I breathe each stroke the painter breathes right through me;
dark, blue dust into the light

of eternal form, he says. So sharp, so cruel, so sensuous
--those eyes like an eagle's.

Is this old man spying or soaring through his own, blue night sky
of sight when he paints me?

Oh, I am exhausted, but those eyes.   Those eyes.

EDGAR DEGAS' "ECOLE de DANSE," 1873

Degas' school at dance begins with a thud.

His drop kick of black-brown, velvet vertical curtain, wall-high,
pounds straight down into an acute angle
to boot
the billowy white butt of the bent-over ballet dancer
below
the bow of her pink sash.

To start the show, is this Degas' bum joke about how high
a French derriere can stick up in the air?

Mais non.
The downbeat points out the bow as the cartwheel center
of his whirl of white
skirts, spinning even as they sit and stand and stretch, starched
white swivelling down the spiral stairs
into
the half-drawn curtain's floor board rush
of window-warm light.

Now your own legs are loosening faster, faster around and around
two pink-tied strings
as the artist's serpentine swirl swings
lower right
up a red shawl slung across another dancer's seated shoulders,
her toe shoes pointed out
in conversation
you're sure you almost over-hear as you twist by.

Your arms are now twirling high above your head and way above
your high hopes
for the grace and poise your lithe body used
to pose
for itself when your life was a dance

and you could step forward each day with joy
in each gesture.

All along the pale-yellow side wall then behind the ponderous
brown pillar, your
circle
surges and churns, wheels and reels
toward the secrets of the master class
hidden in back
around the corner behind the sharp dark curtain where
all butter-glows golden and where Degas has
you
dancing, dancing, dancing, dancing, dancing
toward light.

EDGAR DEGAS' "DANCERS in PINK"

Everything converges in the small of her back:
a sinewy calyx
for flounced-pink skirts, festooned forest scenery leaves,
a background dark brown wedge of stage floor,
and bare-skinned upper bodies
cool
as custard chrysanthemums.

She is one of five pink dancers blooming upright,
their root-legs rooted straight
as stems.

All are stopped-spinning sepals on the painter's pinwheel
of cotton-candy stillness
unless
she pivots
and mixes his palette's bright metaphor
into an even more precious
concoction.

Her fine supple spine
stands erect the entire florid structure of posed, poised action
barely
but long enough gaily in pink
to avoid
rank sentimentality

only through the flesh-pink power of human muscle
tensed.

HENRI MATISSE'S "THE DINNER TABLE (HARMONY in RED),"
1908

I.   Upper Right: Arabesque, Vase, and Woman Bending

If you dance the dance of Matisse's arabesques, your eyes will
dance the divisions

of his classical choreography of squares: the mythical number
four: four-square in four
squares
of dominant design.

In this quadrant, his arabesque spins your first look around
and around its curves

like blue-flaming fingers, like antlers, like the hourglass-eight
shape of woman, like the arc of her bending back,

bending up black back toward blue around these blue baskets
of black-blue flowers,

as they leap, pin-wheel helter-skelter, push and pivot through
their own French countryside of red wallpaper, dish on pedestal,
and its glass vase

with white flowers spraying out over an identically red tablecloth
of flattened space.

The pencil-thin bounding line between table and wallpaper holds
your glance momentarily,
then steps lively back into Matisse's massive
whirl of red,

dancing itself between, out from, then beyond its own borders
of blue lines, lines

in their own red air of static motion that pushes mass
into depthless planes

of more red air,
then even more red air than you can see or breathe,
in this breathless place that gives you even more room to dance.

II.   Lower Right: Plate of Fruit, Two Wine Decanters, and Arabesques

To eat at this table, you must juggle the fruits and buns
like Christmas lights

hanging throughout an invisible red tree of place
above
four more branches of blue arabesques.

The fruit may not all be fruit, these spheres of red, yellow, green,
and orange.

They could be eggs.   It doesn't matter.   They are ornaments.

Hanging from the upward thrust of two wine decanters, from the
flat fir-tree forms of triangles, which will not let them egg-roll
on to the floor.

Three. Three.   Three.   --even more mystical numbers:
a Holy Trinity of corners, sparkling

with the invisible visible energy of spirit-angles, centering
the centerless
center
of Matisse's carnival cartwheel of constant color.

Pick an orange off one of the branches. Put it on your plate.
Matisse has started serving.
The painter invites you to pour the wine and dance.

III.   Lower Left: Rush-Woven Chair

I know you tried to pull this chair up to the table, but it doesn't
move.

You can't sit down on it.   It is not a chair.   It faces forward
forever, away from where your eye wants to rest.

It is a carrot-orange, square-thatched anchor (matching
the woman's orange-carrot hair)

for the lower left back of this square-backed segment
with its four left-moving horizontal
back-slats,

half-in, half-out of the picture, and brightly anchored, anchoring
the frame.

Here, you don't have time to sit.   Get back up.   Matissse draws
you back to dance back up these ladder-slats and out the window.

IV.   Upper Left: Window and Landscape

Outside is inside this window frame, where Matisse's fourth frame
frames nature briefly long enough to resume his basic dance, but

cooler, calmer, less red, no less joyous.

Three tree-clouds billow white and blow, as their black branches
bend and bow

on a background of green green grass under one pink house
and blue sky.

This, not the carrot chair, is your place to rest a minute
from raddish red: to catch your breath

before dancing leaves, dancing on a dancing bush, rustle you
back inside for dinner,

before Matisse's nimble wind winds in and out,
circles and sweeps and sways its magic harmonies through cool air
and arabesques

outside
then circles back inside to dance again,

where Matisse's festive table percolates always alive in line
and color,

where forever Matisse celebrates this busy fussy feast
with gusto and with grace.

MARC CHAGALL'S "BOUQUET and RED CIRCUS," 1960

Paradise is canvas-covered.

Angels wear party hats, play
violins.
A cherub trumpets out balloons.

From the firmament, bounds
the trapeze clown
ringside
in a somersault of flowers.

Yet nowhere in Genesis have I seen
exegesis of this
bare-back nude girl
painting
her lover with light.

All bounces.

Revelation swings into fanfare.

Chagall draws the applause.

MARC CHAGALL'S "FIANCEE with BOUQUET," 1977

A hurrah is the hoop of flowers in her hands,

which she would jump through if only Chagall could draw
a narrower bounce.

Riding bareback, however, she uncoils the penis shaft
of the horse's head with no ears

with plenty of lift

right in front of a curious crowd of peasant houses
which open their eyes wide

at the fiery flames from her fingers.

Red   red   red   red   red   red   red   red   red   red red
is the background of her bouquet:

a drumroll of color,

announcing one more time for all eternity that she enters
the hectic wishing-ring of budding
husbandry,
hope, love, and the burning passion of possibility,
even joy, which
we sketch and resketch for ourselves
over and over,
until daily detail doodles our reddest and most orange
of dreams.

Chagall knows this.

His palette cheers our innermost eye.

His magician-angel hangs a green globe with a yellow streak
in a crimson sky,
outstretched above the crescent moon

of her open arms
for a laugh,
then conjures up a chuckle of crazy characters,
entering from four corners
of this sawdust stage:
acrobat, violin clown, mother with child, musician and lover
(floating upward out of the horse's mane).

If God used Noah, an ark, and twelve tribes to create his parade,
all Chagall needs is a brass band.

MARC CHAGALL'S "BOUQUET with FLYING LOVERS," 1934-47
(painted on a picture underneath, entitled "The Lovers")

In the beginning, the earth was a background without form
or flowers.

Blue did not divide Night from Day, morning from
evening, or three still-life spheres
from a crowded circumference of Russian village
side-shows.

Purple did not yield forth, upper
left, this hidden, crimson-faced cupid, drawing a bow
across the shape
of his body
that is a yellow violin with clown shoes.

In a right lower corner, no pea pod black boat rows an olive bridge
over it, horizontally, into vases of lilies, roses, and lilacs,
to keep them
from spilling a heavenly shaft of moonglow
downward
into chaotic composition.

If these two lovers, floating above the large vase's tilted garden
of red, white, and green impasto,
his arm gently stroking her streaming
,white bridal veil,
ever tasted
of the tree of knowledge of good and evil,

Chagall would never erase
the menacing cock with the cubist eye,
about to announce
that the dawn of their bodies is no longer their dream.

His vision is too real.

Chagall would draw the flying lovers his bouquet-trapeze
out of thin air,
and open wider this nightmare pair
of picture-window frames,
then swing them both east of Eden

where flowerless knowledge is powerless
before ecstasy

and where God paints over the same scheme
twice.

THOMAS HART BENTON'S "PERSEPHONE," 1939

"The nude is stark naked."
--Mary Ellis, pastor, protesting a similar painting by Benton,
6 February 1939

Damn right she is. Stark as I could paint her. Jay-bird naked.
Buck-naked. Bare-ass naked.
Naked as your Aunt Nellie's noodles on her wedding night.

Midwest Missouri mule--hey, I'm one!--naked. Nature-naked.
Goddess-naked.
Naked as the sultry spirit of spring that she becomes when
she shoots
up out each year from Hades,
off Pluto's underworld two-mule wagon, upper right, up to earth
to curl men's toes
and peel the skin right off the grapes
on this vine of curling leaves.

The bright bare light from her skin arches her curves bending
curves into the river
bend in a lush landscape of the midwest land of harvest
wheat and the bountiful plenty
she provides.

That old man leering at her in darkness above the labial log
will want to have
what he's merely dreamed
--the mystery, the magic, the grace of Woman--
never before seen with naked beauty
this naked.

He is my hillbilly father having, slamming my Texas
mother's elegant bedroom door
shut at night so often in my childhood despite her screams
in protest.

The pastor said,"degrading, insult to womanhood--pure filth"?

Not she.   He.

My critics charge, "sensual, gross, profane and vulgar"?
Some want to bar my naked nudes from the City Art Museum
in St. Louis.

Well, I did say my pictures hang better in saloons
than art houses.

My opinion? My dang painting.   Me stubborn?   Missouri Mule?
I showed an ancient myth
of power to the Show Me State. Call me the goddamn Harry Truman
of American art.

Gave 'em hell,
Harry!

THOMAS HART BENTON'S "BUTTERFLY CHASER," 1951

Dad, another painting?   I mean I like it. I love it. You give me one
every birthday.
(I was hoping for a Schwinn!)

It's very nice.   Just a few questions. That's right:
your twelve-year old daughter Jessie
--the   kid-critic--
seeking out the father painter's
secrets.

I know I'm the butterfly chaser,
but why are the butterfly and I so small and everything
else
so big and dark and squirmy?
I mean it's my present. I'm the one who should be big
at twelve and taller.

Are those jaws opening in the brown-black furry-curly forest
ready to swallow
my white butterfly and white net?
Me too?

Is this long low limb an elephant or tree trunk with two branches
like devil's horns
sticking out the snout? It has an eye, I think. Should I climb on,
feed it peanuts, or run away and join
the circus?

Is this stringy, snakey vine a jump rope, swing set, sling shot,
or wishbone? Should I make a wish?
Should I wish to jump rope to thirteen before this
picture eats me alive for its picnic
lunch?

No, I'm not scared.   It's fun. Just a little strange, Dad,
and warm, warming, breathing.

These reds and yellows glow like coals from a volcano I saw
in far away geography
at school.
The flowers and ferns so alive I know they flow
from your egg tempera and oil paint but look
like lava leaves.

Why two tan-tone circles, this open shoe and empty tin can,
one on each side
of the swollen base of the rock-hard,
upward-pointing gray
petrified wood?
Why is the point pointing toward me?

Is this blue shape a lake or a hole to fall through
to heaven or hell?
Why do I begin to feel this painting all over my body?

I'm liking it more and more, Dad. This present is mine.

Last question:
what happens when I catch the butterfly?

PRE-RAPHAELITE SWANS

As they bend their necks to the shimmering mirror
that is the pond,
their reflection is a bright blue ripple of sapphire, delicately
ringing the shore
of bull rushes that bend the wind
whichever way
they choose to sigh in its direction.
Scallops of water from four web-footed paddles reenamel
the placid surface of appearance
with two wakes of thin waves so delicate they will never break
the decorative image long enough to
breach
any sandy bank
of archaic romantic habitation.

Cloud-white is less trite a way to gloss this blue hue
and view of watery illusion

that crosses and criss-crosses,
where foam-white wings feed and carress
in pairs
of eggshell-ivory, rowing against an even more idyllic blue that
your intoxicating eye regards as real
as rain.

How could this have ever been the way nature once thought itself
expressed?
How could such thought still be thought
to be
the golden dawn?

This is beyond the issue of artifice.
This is beyond the issue of vapor-dimmed, antique joy.

Lover by imaginable lover, the swans sail pale waters
beneath a shadowy hazel grove.

Their dreams are wandering stars, numberless
in rediscovery
of
wine-stained radiance
and twilight texture so rich it suffocates itself in violet air.

A surging spread of wings suddenly startles the circumscribed
center of the spectacle,
briefly awakening the myth that lies
beast-sleeping
below
any further wish to drown
some counter-revelation in this pastoral pool
of poetry.

How can there ever be room again for such wild sweetness
in our world?

Yeats is dead.

ALBERTA McCLOSKEY'S PAINTING
"STILLIFE, ORANGES with VASE," 1889

Glowing like the California Gold Rush, it's all about
wrapping and unwrapping:

it is exquisitely more than true luxury to contemplate
the delicate paper
that Alberta McCloskey peels back,
crescent by crescent,

as each fold and crease and twist and rip
crisply snow-bursts out
from
sheath-white, blossom-thin tissue
to shine all over
these sundry California-kissed sun-nuggets of rind and pulp
that juice up her sweetening vision
of this 1880s "exotic"
fruit,

squeezed fresh
from tubes that paint an orange

Wild Wild West.

FRANCISCO GOYA'S PAINTING "The BEWITCHED
(PRIEST POURING OIL on the DEVIL'S LAMP)," 1798

You--painter--hear me, you deaf Spaniard!

Do I stretch this silver cruet so far from my sleeve
to pour oil like sacred wine,
or to stop from singeing my black soul like my black robes
on the devil's flame?

Do I cup my hand over my mouth in horror to escape swallowing
smoke,
or to silence my shout that I no longer serve
my beloved Savior?

Why did you draw three dark
wild-eyed, rearing mules, their front hooves swollen
and thrashing above my head,
as they bray forth sickly amber shadows?

How is it
the devil has muscled human arms, extending below
his soot-stained wing and rams horns,
to accept my oily offering?

Ought I petition the Lord here or some similar monster
in a different costume?

Am I the raving raven image of sounds only you can hear
inside
your throbbing head
--those demons in your ears, growing louder and louder
since your own great sickness?

My God, my God,
why have you forsaken me to such infectious furies!

Why am I so frantic to fuel the lamp
of night?

FRANCISCO GOYA'S PAINTING "WITCHES SABBATH," 1798

They offer their emaciated children
even though one infant is already a skeleton, prostrate
on the ground
below three others
which hang in a row skewered like scrumptious Spanish
shiskebab
from a pole that pierces
up
toward the waning cresent moon.

As heaven's black bats swoop down out of night clouds of chaos,
I accept these living babes as tokens
--starving
dolls in skull caps,
tendered by their living mothers--
to the laurel
festooned about my horns.

My goat's whiskers and cloven hooves stand erect above these
faithful
to orchestrate their unbroken circle of devotion,
as they sing my praises from their songs of sabbath
in this Sunday service,
where life and death dance around
my open arms.

FRA ANGELICO'S "THE ARCHANGEL GABRIEL ANNUNCIATE,"
ca. 1430

GABRIEL

Hallelujah?   Hallelujah?
Show me any serious angel with curly orange hair
--and that "heavenly" tunic: hot renaissance pillow-pink!
Standard-issue Italianate gold trim all over
"my" sleeves and halo.
Lifted, no doubt, from a flashy fabric bash in Florence in 1430.
Good Lord, I look like an oracle-carrying, harp-winged
Harpo Marx.

I recall myself as a subtler, disembodied essence, a voice
for the ear and heart, carrying a message
of fruitfulness to the barren
and the virginal:

"Thou has found favour with God to conceive in thy womb,
and bring forth a son."

That woman then took upon faith what her brother-in-law
Zacharias found sceptical about his years-stricken
wife Elizabeth,
so I struck him dumb.

If I had a face, I would state that the artist has caught
in those flashing eyes some of the glory
of the moment
and the serious force of my salutation.

I presume this is what happens when men try to paint the Word
of joy and glad tidings.

FRA ANGELICO

O spiritual literalist, your protestant protest knows at least
about portraits that, to paint words,
one must look beyond ornament to the hands and eyes.

There you will find the eternal office
of angels and annunciations, even as speechless Zacharias,
his tongue
finally loosened from your aggressive admonition,
prophesied my mission in words about his own
only son John the Baptist:

"To give the knowledge of salvation unto his people . . .
To give light to those that sit in darkness."

GABRIEL

Peace, painter.
We both stand in the presence of God.

ANNA GELLENBECK'S PAINTING
"RICHARDSON HIGHWAY, ALASKA," 1944

It looks more like a seascape, this surf-burst
of sun-bright clouds,

breaking like some cataclysmic conch over the barren landscape
of Alaska, from a cold cool dawn
of lavender and yellow-white light, bright
as pearls.

Who would ever think this blossoming orchid of an oyster shell
could ever flower-flood high above
a frozen desert road,
weary
with tundra?

Anna Gellenbeck.

RIVER LANDSCAPE in MIST with GEESE and FLOCKING CROWS

Chinese handscroll, ink on silk: Chao Ling-jan
c. A.D. 1070-1100

Not this. Not this. Not this gateless gate.

O the river-path that winds around this watery land washes
up through
the sweeping scythe of crows into a single stream,
rushing the river bend into sky
beyond
the grassy brush strokes of refreshing negation.

The mist is not this.

Not this the crows' arc of wings that flow far above the swimming
geese
about to fly
through the same mist that cuts the standing line of firs
into half and air.

Not anything,
not mist is grasped between the finger-branches
of the drooping willow tree, drooping to balance the left shore
from the black, back-draft thrust of flocking
crows.

When you take your first step into the watery way, step first into
the marsh of clouds
flooding the base of the river; the geese will then dance and dive
above and below the surface of nature's mirror of mist
to prepare you to take
the path
through the gate that will never close.

Glide forward on these shimmering surfaces; skim the negated
particulars

57

which open and shut like hollow reeds
drifting stiller and stiller,
still
with the current.

As you follow the black-bright flashing flight of crows, let go
your faintest hopes.

Not this. Not this.

Now you are empty enough for a breathless splash
of ready rapture.

AUTUMN GRASSES

Japanese, six-panel screen on gold ground, early Edo period,
mid-17th century

The path to find the clear way of each wind lies beyond the shapes
of slight stalks.
It is too much assertion, even, to notice how
the ghost of dry tassels
flutter inside brittle, unemptied direction.

No matter their cracked finger-skins or billowy, web-fine
fragility, these gnarled husks
are far too tangible
a source to locate the true place of lush stillness.

You must look between the long, brown and green leaves,
bent thin-back
between eternity and annihilation
for what is left
from your vision of the past year now past all seeking.

In these suggested, stopped spaces, purple plum grass recedes
from jade-cool desire
upper right into the back corner panel, pushing
its larger low counterpart left in and out
of two dimensions
until the winds of no-motion blow their fresh flat breezes
wholly up
against the grain of self-composition.

Now middle stems dance their sprigs and sprays behind and back
over silent shadows
in golden, ancient arcs of smooth spirit,
smooth
as the breath of life,
as thinking of nine ways of doing nothing,

as focusing the mind into one uncarved block that, if named,
shatters into
too many vessels,
to kill the Buddah when you meet him.

Now you are almost free from fresh flowers.

Now your third eye opens to the true, graceful vision of autumn
grasses
--a stationary swirl of sweet serenity, empty
and emptying clearer
and closer
until you are left with the still quiet joy
of
nothing near.

SWALLOWS and APRICOT BLOSSOMS

Chinese Hanging Scroll, Silk Tapestry, Ming Dynasty

You can't count the ways of water
that follow over flow and through the blue-purple porous rock
of trying times, mushrooming
up
--an   iron-wrought,   iris-shape--
from earth,
all filled with holes.

There are always nine ways too many
to number.

The streams of surge unseen configure nature's sacred circles
in this pair of swallows,
bending the backs of their sweet wings
around the quiet whirl of apricot blossoms
dancing,

and in
the bending back around
of branches of the gnarled tree
of consonant wisdom,
as its petals grapple upward toward
space and sun
dancing.

Beneath them both, evergreen bamboo shoots also learn
to bend up into life
but not to break the outline
of the winter of
drab
experience.

This season too is necessary, for its cold flow of flurries
mirrors winter's frigid waters

hardening past growth into ice and spring,
melting

fresh for now
before early snow falls again all along
the numberless ways
of
One attainable path.

POPPIES

Japanese painting on gold paper, mid-17th century

Float down and up, and up above the ground
to tell me what you've found. Push back, pull back the dark green
jungle of leaves below behind each pod to find
that the flailing tiger of desire
hides beneath a flashing foliage of weeds, gnashing its teeth before
your face
while you search.

If you continue to seek,
the red and white petals will also continue to stretch
above their stems.

Their leaves will curl your blank bleak urgency of needs
up out from within yourself in black-jade folds
of ascending weightless gesture. Here is the ultimate
opiate.

Here fan-shaped leaves fight flight
only long enough
to stand and swirl effortlessly beyond base earth toward sky.

Elevation now flows from momentary stoppage toward a realm
you always knew you could find
but lost sight from too much possession.

When each poppie blossoms each of its own petals into nothing,
your trance dances lighter and higher
between
affirmation and negation,
and the prison stripes on the tiger's tail turn you
all the way around toward
another Way.

Your third eye now sees that your vantage is altitude,
and that poppies are mountain tops capped with snow and sunset

--are candles blown out farther up where
mist
empties attachment and assertion
into perfect wisdom
as you climb

lighter and higher, higher and lighter.

THALIA

suggested by Jean-Baptiste Regnault's painting
"The Three Graces," 1793

Ungirdled from inner earth outward from glacial fissure
arms entwined above
hair streaming toward the precipice, she pauses,
bows to me as usual;
then, lifting her garments slowly one by one
draws taut the tendon behind the knee, and with lithe riband
of upper thigh springs downward over palisade
and shore over riverbank and gorge, provoking me
to the chase
while she spirals, pivots in air laughing at me to enscribe
her at the waist
and pull each other struggling into the tall grass, where
elemental force is found in the imperative
from her hips, where battle is done
with all the fierce back-breaking parts, until no winner
emerges besplendent
with true promise, truly a compromise, though still a grace:
her song, eternally
that of the great River Lord whose grandaughter she is
and is become again at my desire.

HARRIET FOSTER BEECHER'S PAINTING
"A CAMP on the TIDE FLATS," 1897

That black empty iron skillet on the cold fire,
two or three
woven baskets, the tent tarp almost flapping in the sea breeze,
the skiff beached, its lowered sail pointing
where
an Indian Woman peers out over the tide flats,
her black hair pulled back,
her unseen eyes
anchored

to horizon upon horizon of brackish salt air,
watching
and
waiting and watching.

CLARISSE MADELENE LAURENT'S PAINTING "EGGS," 1892

Not so academic as you think:
this pewter teapot, five egg yolks floating on a pale plate, broken
egg shells carefully cupped inside
each other,
a small fork, prongs pointing properly down,
and a leafy green garnish--all ready
to scramble.

Sweet peas.   Sweet peas.   Sweet peas.

MARION CANFIELD SMITH'S PAINTING "A CORN FIELD," 1920

Corn stalks,
standing sentinel so stern against cool autumn wind,
bend close to overhear
me
just as the earth rushes past
your gusty breeze
of
a pumpkin
patch.

I am lonely,
and these empty ears of broken corn will not strain
to listen
to the scattering silence
of
my sweet
song.

ABOUT the AUTHOR

Robert Kirschten is the author of <u>James Dickey and the Gentle Ecstacy of Earth: A Reading of the Poems</u>; "<u>Approaching Prayer</u>": <u>Ritual and the Shape of Myth in A.R. Ammons and James Dickey</u>; and three books of poems, <u>Old Family Movies</u>, <u>Chicago Poems</u>, and <u>Looney Tunes: A Comic Book of Poems</u>.

He is the editor of <u>Critical Essays on James Dickey</u>, "<u>Struggling for Wings</u>": <u>The Art of James Dickey</u>, <u>James Dickey: The Selected Poems</u>, and <u>Critical Essays on A.R. Ammons.</u>